# YESTERDAY

# YESTERDAY

## ADÈLE GERAS

**WALKER BOOKS**
LONDON

This book is dedicated to everyone who appears in its pages, with special thanks to David Wood for allowing me to quote from his songs and look at his cuttings, and to Jan Mark for finding the modern equivalent of the Map.

First published 1992 by Walker Books Ltd
87 Vauxhall Walk, London SE11 5HJ

Text © 1992 Adèle Geras

First printed 1992
Printed and bound in Great Britain by
Billings & Sons Ltd, Worcester

British Library Cataloguing in Publication Data
A catalogue record for this book is
available from the British Library

ISBN 0-7445-2105-X

# CONTENTS

# THE MAP

Some people believe in Heaven; my father believed in Paris and Oxford, both of which had the distinct advantage of being easily reached by conventional means of transport. My early childhood was spent in various distant corners of what used to be called the British Empire. All the bits of the atlas that were coloured pink were areas where first King George VI and later Queen Elizabeth II sent my dad.

"I am a Servant of the Queen," he would announce proudly and with capital letters in his voice, though I could see little sign of it. Such a person would surely wear a white wig and knee breeches and a blue uniform encrusted with gold braid, but my father had to wait for his grand attire until he became a judge. Still, he was sent by the Reigning Monarch to Nigeria and North Borneo and the Gambia and Tanganyika. The Public Works Department in every Colony provided us with a house complete with all its furniture: rattan chairs with podgy beige cushions, chests of drawers and cupboards and, of course, The Desk.

The Desk always had three drawers on one side of the knee-hole and three on the other, and a flat top,

like a table. I don't know whether it was PWD policy
or whether my dad thought of it all by himself (No,
it must have been policy. My dad was baffled by tin
openers...), but the writing surface of the Desk was
always covered with a sheet of clear glass and under
it, in every single place to which he was sent, lived
the Map of Oxford, which was one of the chief
delights of my earliest years.

I have just taken the Map out and had a look at
it. Since my father died, it's been mine. I intended
at first to have it framed and hang it on a wall, and
psychologists will say that the reason I haven't done
so for nearly twenty years is because I do not wish
to be constantly reminded of my father and my
vanished childhood. They may well be right, but I've
got an even simpler reason. It's because memories of
the Map are better than the real thing.

When I was small, it seemed huge. I used to sit at
my dad's desk and look in the drawers for pipe-cleaners, or shining new blue-lined paper, or shocking-
pink shoelace-type ribbon which my dad said was the
famous Red Tape all government departments were
so frightfully keen on. Under my hands as I wrote on
the paper, or twisted the pipe-cleaners into people-
shapes, the Map spread and spread under the glass,
and I used to catch sight of first one bit of it and then
another.

What it shows is Oxford, within a border of the
College Coats of Arms. Beside each heraldic shield
some small figures stand, about three or four to each
College, and these are the famous Old Boys, for this
Map was drawn in the days before Old Girls were
thought of with much respect. These clever people

are generally politicians, bishops, bigwigs of one kind and another, with the odd poet thrown in to spice the procession up a bit. This frieze of the Great and Worthy in their period costume frames a three-dimensional representation of the City itself, and on every street, in every park, beside the river, tiny figures walk. There's Lewis Carroll with Alice in tow, Sir Max Beerbohm with his entrancing heroine, Zuleika Dobson, the Martyrs on their way to the stake, Queen Matilda fleeing, Prince Rupert fighting a duel, a Dane looking as if he's about to leap over the river in his frenzy, and on the water itself, a minuscule "eight" of fair-haired young chaps, having a jolly good row in a teeny-weeny boat.

Just as Heaven-believers have a vivid mental picture of, say, serried ranks of white-robed cherubim, clouds, harps and gates of pearl, I had a clear idea of Oxford based on this wonderful Map. I saw the real place for the first time in 1962 when I went there for my interview, but by then I'd been a believer in Oxford-as-paradise for ten years or more. My father had been quite right about Paris, where we went almost every year, so I gave him the benefit of the doubt in the matter of universities or, as he preferred to call them: "Varsities".

He'd studied Law at Pembroke College in the early thirties and didn't really think there *was* such a thing as another university. If there was, it was the Sorbonne in Paris and certainly not Cambridge: that outcrop of college-like edifices set in the dank heart of a soggy East Anglian fen, whose only function, as far as my dad could see, was to provide opposition in the Boat Race and the Varsity Matches.

I didn't care much at first. When I say I was a
believer in Oxford I mean only a believer in the
physical place, as I'm now a believer in Venice,
Florence, New Orleans and various other places I've
visited only in my dreams and imaginings. I certainly
never considered Oxford as an Educational Place
because I had only one desire in my early teens, and
that was to go to RADA (Royal Academy of Dramatic
Art), or another drama school, and become a STAR.

I began my pursuit of stardom singing "Black-
eyed Susie" and "You Made Me Love You" at a Red
Cross concert in Jesselton, North Borneo. I was nine.
I was the kind of child who, when asked to perform
by indulgent relatives, would open my mouth to sing
and not close it until some food came along to
distract me. At school I was in the choir and acted
in every school play I could wangle myself into and,
in the summer of 1963, just before going to Oxford,
I had a Brilliant Career in Paris as a busker on the
streets of the Left Bank.

This book is going to be a scrapbook of my memories. What I write may be unreliable, but I shall try
and make it as true as I can. I don't want anyone
pointing out that no, three shillings and ten pence
for twenty was not the price of Nelson cigarettes in
1964. I don't care if it wasn't. 3s. 10d. for twenty is
what I remember, and I have to emphasize most
strongly and loudly here and now that *my memory
may be at fault.* I'm not lying. It's just that every
pair of eyes looks out on a different physical uni-
verse, and every mind looks in at a unique interior
landscape.

The result of this will be: things may not have

happened when I say they did, but I don't think that matters too much. There are two fixed points: I went up to St Hilda's College, Oxford, to read French and Spanish in October 1963 and left in June 1966. A few events during those years can be dated reasonably accurately and, like a person crossing a stream on a series of stepping stones, I shall make my way across this time.

"A book," said Virginia Woolf, "is not made up of sentences laid end to end, but of sentences built ... into arcades and domes." The architectures of fiction are not a bit like our lives which, for the most part, consist of days laid end to end: more a long, dull corridor than elegant arcades etc. At school I tried once to keep a diary, but gave up when I realized that a second helping of rhubarb crumble was often the high point of the week. "Got up. Had lessons. Did Prep. Went to bed," was what my diary looked like on good days. On bad days you might find: "Had a quarrel with X. Got C– for Maths. Rained all day." Life is baggy and shapeless, but books shouldn't be. This is my excuse for leaving certain things out altogether, like the hours and hours of time pleasurably wasted being silly: giggling, lying about on the bed nattering about this and that, loafing around, fooling about. I did an awful lot of that, one way and another.

I should say a word before I begin about the people in these pages. I've decided that the easiest thing to do is call everyone by her or his real name and leave out all surnames, except for those of my teachers. In this way, my friends and acquaintances will either recognize themselves or not. It doesn't much matter as there are going to be no Scandalous Revelations, so anyone wishing to read of Wicked Goings-On can look in another book. Any resemblance between the people in these pages and real people is honest but not complete ... and the picture of myself that I present is probably no nearer to the truth than the one I paint of anyone else.

# GETTING THERE

Tourists stepping off the train at Oxford station and wandering into the town are known to ask, "Where is the university?" and to look somewhat bemused when the Oxford native waves a vague hand to include the whole city. There is not one single building, or set of buildings, which makes up the University – no campus, as in many other places. Rather there are colleges scattered through the town, some of them right on the main streets, others of them hidden away, and it is in these colleges that the students live, and eat at least some of their meals. Nowadays most colleges are co-educational, but in 1962 there were only five women's colleges. I chose to apply to St Hilda's because I knew from the Map that it was:

a) the nearest college to the centre of town and therefore the most convenient for a non-cyclist like me, and

b) on the river.

The system of work was as follows: there were lectures, which were optional. A list would go up at the beginning of term and you could look at it and see if any exciting speakers were appearing, and if there was a lecture that you liked the sound of, you could go to it whether it was in your subject or not. Then there were tutorials. These meant a weekly meeting with your tutor, at which you read an essay aloud which she/he had set you to write the week before. Sometimes tutorials were shared with another person. Generally your tutor lived in your college, but if there was no one on the premises who could teach your subject, then you were "farmed out" to someone in another college. It was thus that I had my Spanish tutorials with a tutor from a man's college. In addition to lectures and tutorials there were odd classes scattered throughout the week for the doing of such things as translation. When you first arrived in your college you were also given a Moral Tutor to whom you could turn if there were any problems.

There is also a kind of uniform which students at Oxford wear on formal occasions. This is called subfusc and consists of (for women) a black skirt, a white blouse, a black tie and black tights. On top of all this, a black sleeveless gown is worn. Most gowns are short and come to just below the waist. They are called Commoner's gowns. Anyone who has a scholarship, though, wears what looks like a traditional teacher's gown as seen in the pages of *Beano*, and these are called Scholar's gowns. As well as the added status these confer, they make very useful dressing-gowns in an emergency. These garments used to be compulsory for all tutorials, lectures and classes, and were worn over one's ordinary clothes.

In 1962 there was only one way to get into Oxford or Cambridge and that was by sitting, in the November after your A levels, a series of very competitive and gruelling exams. Then a shortlist of people was

summoned to interviews at extremely short notice.
Telegrams were sent and you were expected to get
on a train within a couple of days. After the interview you had to wait and then more telegrams
appeared, but only to tell you that you were suc-
cessful.

Imagine me, then, in my last year at boarding-
school. I have made a deal with my dad. I will go
back to school for one term after taking my A levels
and sit the Oxbridge entrance exams. If I fail to get
in my parents have undertaken to pay my way
through drama school. If I do get in there will be
many, many opportunities to act. I know this
because word has returned to school via my friend
Hilary (who played Cauchon to my de Stogumber in
*Saint Joan*), who is now at Cambridge and has
joined the Footlights and seems to do nothing but
act.

It wasn't only Hilary who reconciled me to the
idea of trying for Oxbridge. Michael was a Major
Factor. I fell in love with him during the Christmas
holidays before my A levels. I met him at a party
given by Hilary, or a friend of Hilary's – I no longer
remember. He was my idea of absolute perfection:
immensely tall, painfully thin, very clever indeed
and given to talking about T.S. Eliot as though he
and the poet were best mates. He even quoted *Four
Quartets* as we danced. Is it any wonder that I know
vast tracts of them by heart? I went back to school
bewitched and wrote poems about long fingers, and
practised signing my name with his surname all over
my Rough Book. He was at Cambridge with Hilary.
He acted. He sent me a postcard from Germany

where he was on tour with some student production. The card became thin because I clutched it to my bosom so much and took it out and handled it so often.

As sometimes happens when one is totally besotted, I also fell in love with his family, his house, his street, his entire world, and especially a blonde friend of his called Simon, who looked like Rimbaud (my favourite poet) and was quiet and enigmatic. In April Michael happened to kiss me under a magnolia tree, and back at school this experience emerged as a poem in which I compared magnolia flowers with candles. I went to watch him play cricket at a place called Claygate and, although details of the game are lost, I can remember snogging all the way back to Victoria. There were no modern open-plan trains then, oh no indeed ... this was in the days when one could have an empty compartment, and draw down the blinds.

Even as I sat the Oxbridge exams I could feel Divided Loyalties, not to mention Tugs-of-Love, approaching with all speed.

Michael was at Cambridge, but then there was the Map, and my father, and years of propaganda about the Other Place that even idyllic walks along the Backs with my beloved and drinks at the Eagle could do little to dispel. My resolve might have weakened, I might have tossed Dad, the Map and evil rumours about Cambridge out of the window with a fine and careless rapture for the sake of Love, but Michael did very little to encourage me. He was a rare creature indeed: a Cambridge man who was nevertheless a fervent Oxford-believer. His reason for being one was personal and tragic. An elder, dearly-loved sister at Oxford had been killed in a car accident shortly before I'd met him. He said, "I don't think I'd be able to turn down a place at Oxford."

Also (and I think I may have known this even then, though I managed to push it firmly to the back of my mind so that it no longer existed except as a small, miserable niggle that occasionally surfaced in the dark hours), he certainly didn't love me in the way I loved him, and was probably dreading me appearing in Cambridge to dog his every footstep.

THE SUIT

I was allowed an afternoon off from school to go to town and buy myself a suit for my interviews. My mother, who has wonderful taste, was far away in what had been renamed Tanzania, and left to my own devices, I ended up with a soberly-cut affair: straight skirt (straight skirts are slimming, aren't they?) and plainish jacket (didn't all the magazines advocate simplicity, the classic, timeless elegance ... blah-de-blah?) but all in an eye-blistering emerald green with the subtlety of plastic grass. Well, I thought, green suits me. Looking back, I can see I must have seemed like a rather sturdy leprechaun, an extra from a bad production of *Finian's Rainbow*, but at the time I sincerely thought I was knocking them for six with my stunning apparel.

I bought myself some cigarettes at the station on the way to each of my interviews. I felt grown-up. I read through my French and Spanish textbooks on the train, making sure the covers were visible to everyone. I wanted all the other passengers to know where I was off to, to realize what an exceptional person was travelling with them. No one even looked at me, of course. To them I was just a podgy schoolgirl in a pea-pod of a suit.

I went to my Cambridge interview first. I remember very little about my time there except that the building reminded me of school. I walked round a town that was totally empty because Michael wasn't there. It was miles from Girton College to the centre ... how would I ever get there and back? I didn't know how to ride a bike, and I congratulated myself again for choosing St Hilda's as my Oxford college.

Of my Oxford interview, more than anything I remember the bells, ringing out from this tower and that, all through the night. The room I stayed in was in a building called Hall, which looked out on to the river. I liked St Hilda's immediately. There was a wonderful sweeping staircase in Hall, and the rooms were high-ceilinged and quiet, and everyone else at the interview seemed friendly. I met a girl called Helen, who came from London and looked very clever. How do you look clever? Well, you are thin and intense, and having dark hair helps, and the finishing touch is purple smudges under your eyes. It's hard to appear a diamond-sharp intellectual with a chubby round face and rosy cheeks.

Helen and I walked around Oxford and I fell in love. I recognized famous landmarks from the Map, but nothing – not the Map, not my dad's descriptions, not Gerard Manley Hopkins' poem – nothing had prepared me for the physical beauty of the town. I walked around with my mouth open and my neck twisted round and up, trying to take in everything at once. By the time we got back to College for supper, I'd decided. This was where I wanted to be, and so much so that I'd have been very upset if I'd had to go to Cambridge or RADA instead.

I lay awake half the night listening to the bells, and on the train on the way back to school, I wrote a poem about them.

Michael was unflatteringly philosophical when I told him I wouldn't be going to Cambridge after all. He said he would visit me at College. It was around this time, I think, that a St Hilda's undergraduate was sent down for dallying with a don in her bedroom. There was even a Giles cartoon about it. Nothing happened to the gentleman, which struck us even then as most unfair. I felt I was very adult to be going to a place where such things occurred. I had been awarded a scholarship (and so had Helen) and was therefore entitled to the long, black gown. I thought I would look dashing and striking.

I sent a telegram to my parents with the good news, and found it carefully folded into my father's papers after his death ten years later. My mother told me it had remained stuck in the frame of his shaving mirror for months.

# OXFORD

When I arrived at Oxford, it was a city of pale grey and creamy gold ancient buildings, spires, gargoyles, rotundas, columns, arches and bridges. It was a city of pinkish Victorian brick and modern glass and the crumbling stone faces of the Roman emperors outside the Sheldonian Theatre. It was a place of rivers and walled gardens and more shades of green than you could number. It was full of shops: the one where Alice met a sheep knitting was just down the road from Marks and Spencers, Woolworths and the Kardomah Café. I liked a special kind of Oxford shop which sold college scarves, mortar boards and gowns and the kind of pastel woolly jumper never seen outside advertisements for golfing equipment, and headgear to be worn only while killing various forms of wildlife. There were bookshops everywhere. Walking down Broad Street (which is called the Broad), you sensed the hidden streams of writing and still more writing piled up in the stacks of the Bodleian Library, down there beneath your feet. There was a covered market with a wonderful café called George's, where you could get breakfast if you failed to get up in time for what your college was offering.

The central part of Oxford is small, and that means it's easy to walk around, but – and it's this that keeps the town from becoming one enormous Ivory Tower and enables it to be counted as part of the Real World – Oxford is also an important centre of the car manufacturing industry, which means that there's a population walking around that is separate from students and their teachers.

And then of course, there were the King's Arms, the Kemp and the Playhouse, of which more later.

THE FIRST DAYS

The room I was given when I arrived at St Hilda's was a mistake. I think it was supposed to be for one of the dons, or if not that, at least for a Third Year student, and not a Fresher. It was enormous, with three big windows looking over the river to Merton College. I wanted to stay there for ever. It was the only room that felt truly mine since I was eleven and first went to boarding-school. That's what we were all called during the first few weeks: Freshers. I found it embarrassing. It emphasized the schooly aspect of college and I thought I had left school for ever. There was the Freshers' Fair, for example, which went on in the Town Hall. I hurried along to it, even before I'd unpacked. Every society in the University had a stall there, and I never knew there could be so many activities, but I ignored the siren voices of the Ramblers, Mountaineers, Chess fiends, Politicos, Sporty Types and Religious ones because I knew where I was going. Women couldn't yet join the Oxford University Dramatic Society (henceforward OUDS), although we were allowed to audition

for the female parts in every production they put on.
This all changed before I left Oxford thanks to the
efforts of some of the undergraduate actresses.
Meanwhile, I joined the Experimental Theatre Club
(ETC) and returned to college exhilarated. I was
going to a Special Meeting for Freshers on Sunday
in Worcester College. I could hardly wait.

Friends of mine have told me how I chattered
away in a loud and confident voice at supper that
first night in college, while they were feeling lonely,
miserable, new and shy, and how I made them feel
even worse. I can't deny it. My voice *is* loud. My
children are for ever ssh-ing me on buses and in
shops, which seems wrong. Aren't mothers supposed
to keep their kids quiet? Anyway, I apologize in
retrospect, as it were, and have to admit that because
I'd been so used to school, this really *did* seem only
an extension and not a great change at all. After supper, a kind Second Year student made us cocoa in
her room. She was very nice. Everyone was very
nice, but I decided that cocoa was not what universities were supposed to be about. I had been to the
Freshers' Fair. I had a meeting to go to. I would
meet people. I would meet Men.

MEN
There were seven men to every woman in Oxford
during my time there. Of course, they were not evenly
distributed. Some beauties had fourteen or more
while others went without entirely, or that's what it
sometimes looked like. I was still in love with
Michael, therefore the pursuit wasn't quite so urgent,
but he was There and I was Here and I wasn't going

to go about with my eyes closed. Young men were a strange and wonderful species. We had seen very little of them at my school, and everything about them was both mysterious and entrancing. What I liked best was the way shirts hung on their backs, and fell into thrilling folds on their way to the waistbands of jeans. I could see, just from one day in this place, that there were hundreds of the creatures walking round quite freely. I had all the feelings of a zoologist entering a particularly well-stocked jungle.

Because of this ratio of seven to one, the young men newly arrived at their colleges were athirst for even a glimpse of passable girls. The result of this was a pigeon-hole in the porter's lodge crammed full of luscious-looking invitations printed on stiff card. For the first few weeks, I did try and go to as many staircase parties as I could, ever mindful of the lurking cocoa that awaited those who lingered in college after supper.

The first staircase party I ever went to was not a success. It was held in the Oscar Wilde rooms in Magdalen College, which was conveniently next door to St Hilda's, as it were, just over the bridge. There were so many people in those rooms, wreathed in such enveloping fogs of cigarette smoke that no one was visible at all. The music – very early Beatles, Dylan, etc. – was so loud that all witticisms and bright remarks were knocked on the head and thoroughly stunned by the volume, even as they left your mouth. People introduced themselves and you didn't catch their name and then they drifted away and you never saw them again. More than anything it seemed (as it almost always does seem at parties like this, I've since discovered ... oh, the wisdom and understanding that age brings!) *that every single other person in the room was having the time of their life.* I stood crushed against the window frame, unable to reach the door for the press of bodies, consoling myself with the thought that Oscar Wilde himself used to live here, and this was Me, really Me, in his rooms.

A confession. When I was eighteen, I was the star of all kinds of movies that went on in my head. I saw myself constantly as an imaginary camera might see me. As above: Our Heroine, looking alienated and hopefully slightly sultry and shot in grainy black and white ... very Nouvelle Vague. Everywhere I went for the first days at Oxford, I kept saying to myself: this is Me, walking down the High, Me wearing my gown, this is really Me being in a tutorial, going to a meeting of the ETC: Me looking like a real, live undergraduate. I haven't outgrown this childish habit, I'm ashamed to say. When I first went down to London to meet a publisher, and especially when I was taken to lunch, I can remember thinking: this is Me, having lunch with my editor.

MOODS
I have to say a word about the absence of angst, depression, ennui and despair in these pages. I'm generally of a cheerful disposition and equable temperament, and was quite happy for most of the time, even as an adolescent. I sometimes wonder if I'd have turned out haunted and gloomy if I'd been born with cheekbones. I was sad on occasion, of

course, but only with good reason (a boyfriend had dumped me, say) and for a limited period. I always cheered up again as the next prospect appeared on the horizon. If I did a bad essay, I was annoyed or fed up or briefly depressed, but only until the next essay gave me hopes of something better. I'm an optimistic person not only when I think of the future, but also when I look back at things that have already happened to me, so I apologize for not having any desperate miseries worth writing about – they're usually interesting to read.

FRESHERS' PHOTO
There was one day, during those first weeks, when the whole of the first year of St Hilda's College was arranged on the lawn in tidy lines and photographed for posterity. The Class of '63. I am going to arrange a photograph of my own, in order to introduce some people into this narrative. I didn't meet all of them straight away, but by the time I left Oxford, these were most of my friends. In the front row are my college girlfriends: Franny, Liz, Maggie, Chris, Nata, Wendy, Ann and Anne, Tammy. In the second row are my girlfriends from other colleges: Philippa, Marian, Maria, Lynn. In the third row are lots of men I knew and was not romantically involved with: Dick, Bob, Woody, David, Jo, Roland, Simon, Braham, John, Geoff, etc. On the back row (quite a short row, this!) anyone who could qualify as a boyfriend, for however short a time: Hugh, Richard, Iwan, Tim, Vince. I met my husband in 1964. He has a row all on his own.

A few faces in this photograph must be looked at

more closely. Franny was dark, with a pale skin and almond-shaped, amber-coloured eyes, set wide apart. She came from Birmingham, which she claimed was full of ugly people, and she introduced me to Jazz. It was through Franny that I got to know the music of Cab Calloway, Bessie Smith, Lester Young, Duke Ellington and Billie Holiday. Even now, whenever I hear "Edie Was a Lady" or "Minnie the Moocher" I think of her. Franny could make dresses by throwing material on the floor of her room and cutting freehand into the cloth with no pattern to speak of. She was the best dancer I've ever seen. When she got going, you would have sworn there wasn't a bone in her whole body. She had a tendency to fall in love with charming rogues, which made for sleepless nights and red eyes, but plenty of interest.

Liz had long dark wavy hair, with a streak of grey in it, at the front. She had a beautiful, serene face and clothes that seemed to me expensive and properly grown-up in a way I'd never quite managed. Liz was not involved in the theatre, which made her the perfect confidante for gossip. Wendy was pretty, with brown curls around a plump face and wide grey-blue eyes. During the first year, her room was the one we all climbed into to get into Hall after the gates had been locked at midnight. Maggie was blonde and very small, with rosy cheeks. Chris had the cheeky face of an urchin and black hair in a Nefertiti hairdo. Philippa had been at school with me and was now at St Hugh's. I had been envying her eyelashes and huge grey-green eyes since I was twelve. Nata was tall and dark, with very good legs. (A.J.P. Taylor, the eminent historian, used to give her tutorials. When it was decided that women students were allowed to wear trousers with gowns, he asked Nata as a special favour to continue wearing skirts whenever she came to see him. This is the sort of thing that would raise a few eyebrows nowadays, but then ... ah, then we just thought that A.J.P. was being endearingly eccentric.)

They looked like that then. Those of them whom I still see sometimes look just the same to me now as they did twenty-seven years ago: older, thinner, more glamorous, all of them grown up now, but unchanged.

Other names may also appear from time to time. Does it seem like a cast of thousands? Taking part in any theatrical production means that immediately you are involved with a great many others, and I became very committed to a show within days of arriving at Oxford.

MONEY

Having my first bank account went to my head a little. I had never been in charge of my own money before, and I suddenly noticed that the shops were full of desirable objects.

The first thing I bought, from an antique shop quite near to my college, was a large dish made of Carnival glass, which I thought would do for an ashtray. It cost me two pounds and I hesitated outside the window for ages. Two pounds was a lot of money to me then. In the end, I succumbed. I always *do* succumb if I want the thing badly enough, but this dish was a wise choice. I've seen a great deal of antique Carnival glass since then, and this is the most beautiful example: its frilly edges a shimmering orange that looks like silk solidified. I've managed to keep it, unbroken, through various house-moves and it still gives me enormous pleasure.

I also bought a wide-brimmed navy blue hat from BHS. In those days I thought it looked dramatic, especially in conjunction with the dark glasses I favoured a lot of the time, even indoors, and even in the winter. This hat I also have, but for the last seventeen years it has lived with the dressing-up clothes and my children used to use it when they were younger and pretending to be cowgirls.

I fixed up my room with a bedspread of Madras cotton in stripes of purple, pinks and indigos. I hung up some pictures painted by my uncle Reggie who lived in Paris and was a bona fide starving artist, but no one paid them much attention. I equipped myself with a tea-set of pale blue china from Woolworths, ready for tea-parties I imagined would be populated by all the cleverest, handsomest and most interesting people around in the fullness of time. Meanwhile my girlfriends and I would be able to munch biscuits and drink coffee late at night while we picked over the bones of any romance that was currently pre-occupying us.

One day during my second year, I received a letter from my Bank Manager. This terrifying being wished to see me personally. I trembled my way to Lloyds Bank and was ushered into the presence. I knew I was a little overdrawn, but this? The Bank Manager smiled at me.

"I have here," he said, "a letter from the Hon. Mr Justice Weston. Your father," he added unnecessarily.

"Shall I read it to you?"

I nodded, speechless. The letter went something like this ... time has obscured the details, but what it said remains with me still: "Should my daughter's overdraft at any time exceed the sum of thirty pounds, I would be most grateful if you would call her into your office and give her a piece of your mind. You may be as severe as you like ... a jolly good telling-off is what I mean..."

I blushed as the Bank Manager read it. I spent a few minutes describing my father, apologizing for him. We reached the conclusion together that he was a lovable eccentric. Judges often were, weren't they? It went with the job. We parted amicably. I went back to College and wrote a furious letter to my dad. By return I received a cheque for fifty pounds and an exhortation not to forget to brush my teeth, night and morning.

# TOTAL
# THEATRE

The ETC Freshers' meeting was packed. There was hardly room to stand. Jo addressed us, wearing the first black leather jacket I had seen in real life, close up. At first, I thought Jo was very ugly, but within five minutes I'd changed my mind and decided he was the most attractive person in the room. His battered-looking face had been almost completely destroyed in a car crash, and remodelled by skilled plastic surgery. Jo was tall and dark, and spoke with enthusiasm about the show for which all of us Freshers were being asked to audition. It was going to be a new concept: Total Theatre. The Director and Deviser (not Writer) would gather a company around them and from improvisations and workshops a show would be put together in the same way that *Oh, What a Lovely War!* had been assembled by Joan Littlewood and her actors. That had been an anti-war show: the ETC's was going to be an anti-capital punishment one. We were all invited to audition at University College (Univ.).

On the same day that the ETC was auditioning at Univ., across the road at St Edmund Hall someone called Michael (who came from Texas and was said to be nearly as good-looking as Jo) was holding audi-

tions for *Twelfth Night*. Choices had to be made.
Total Theatre was a bit of an unknown quantity, but
I knew *Twelfth Night*. Maria was the only part I
could hope to play, and the chances of there being
no one in the Second and Third Years who was
better than me were so tiny as to be invisible. I opted
for Univ. and, pausing only to admire Shelley's
marble form laid out on a plinth, I made my way to
the audition.

It was held in an enormous room. Braham (the
Director) and David (the Deviser) were sitting at a
table. There may have been others, but they're the
ones I recall. Braham was very thin and dark with a
lugubrious cast of features. He looked at me with sad
brown eyes. People often wondered whether Braham
was cross with them. He was not given to smiling
unnecessarily, and therefore if you made him smile,
you counted it as a triumph. David, sitting next to
him, was beautiful. He had pale, very smooth skin
and hair flopping into his eyes. He pushed it back
constantly with (yes, my favourite!) long, elegant
fingers.

"Right," said Braham, "what can you do?"
I mumbled a bit about past roles at school. Then I
said, "I can sing."

Braham told me to go to the other end of the
room and begin. I sang a Joan Baez song called "El
Preso Numero Nueve" (Prisoner No. 9) because I
thought it was appropriate for a show about capital
punishment.

The main thing that can be said about my voice
is that there is lots of it. It filled the whole of the
room we were in and bounced back off the walls.

Braham and David agreed I would be useful. I was
in. I had a part. The first rehearsal was scheduled for
the next day. I was one of the company of *Hang
Down Your Head and Die* or *Hang* as it was always
called.

THE KEMP
Braham, David, Jo and Michael-from-Texas held
court every morning in a café called the Kemp, on
the corner of the Cornmarket and Broad Street,
above a shop which sold maroon eiderdowns and
fringed lampshades. The *Hang* company and the
*Twelfth Night* company went there as well,
although we didn't often get to sit at the tables of the
Great and Famous. There was friendly rivalry
between the two companies. Michael-from-Texas
sometimes brought Doug and Annabel with him.
They were a Couple: both blonde and immensely
glamorous and playing, respectively, Feste and
Viola. I gawped at them and also at Michael J., who
was playing Sebastian and was going out with a
St Hilda's girl called Juliet. Franny came with me
almost every day, and we sat with Bob, who had
a wonderful baritone voice and who was big and
chubby and kind and chatty, and his friend from
school, Dick, who was sardonic and funny and had
the added cachet of being the younger brother of
Famous Jo, who was also in the cast. We ate anchovy
toast, or cinnamon toast, and teacakes with some of
the lesser members of the cast and with Iwan, who
was in charge of the music.

Occasionally, when there wasn't room anywhere
else, we had to squeeze ourselves on to a table with

Jo, Emrys, Braham or David. Then we didn't say much, but listened to every word. Jo announced one day that the whole key to *Macbeth* was the fact that by the end of the play, Macbeth has not slept for days. Was it any wonder he was seeing things and behaving strangely? This struck me as very perceptive. Jasmina (from Persia) and Hope (from Jamaica) were always at the table too, because they were going out with Braham (Jasmina) and Jo (Hope). I stared at them and wished I could be as gorgeous and exotic as they were. They were in the *Hang* cast as well, and so, most importantly of all, were Woody and Terry.

There was an awful lot of aimless drifting about from one lot of food and drink to another. Mornings at the Kemp often merged and blended imperceptibly into lunch with Bob and Dick in the Buttery at Merton. This was convenient for rehearsals, which were often held in a basement just a short walk down the High, opposite the Eastgate pub.

I was in the Eastgate only once, but that was on the night that President Kennedy was assassinated. Some of us were having a drink there before going to a staircase party at Queen's. Jo came in and told us what had happened and I went back to college. No one felt like going to a party any longer. We watched TV and saw for the first time the images (the long cars, the President rising as the bullets hit him, and Jackie in her pale pink dress all covered with blood) which would be repeated and repeated over the years.

NAMES

At school, my nickname was Delly. During the early days of rehearsing for *Hang*, everyone started to call me "Addle". Anyone who knows me from those days still calls me that, except for my husband, who has never used the name.

WORK – AN INTERRUPTION
While we gossiped theatrical gossip in the Kemp, other people must have been going to lectures, or working in the libraries. I went to tutorials. I went to any classes I absolutely had to go to. I wrote any essays I absolutely had to write, usually after midnight, in a bit of a rush and not having done anything like enough reading. My French tutor was called Mrs Gerard-Davis. Once a week, I would go and sit in her room and peer at her through veils of cigarette smoke (hers and mine) and improvise like mad, thinking up a good reason for not having written an adequate essay. Once, in desperation, I said I couldn't possibly write my essay on Racine as a Classical dramatist because I didn't think he *was* a Classical writer at all, but a Baroque one. Mrs G-D, far from chasing me out of the room with a flea in my ear, said, "How fascinating! Do tell me exactly what you mean. How, for instance, would you define 'Baroque'?"

I wish now I'd had more time to pursue my interest in the Baroque. In Spanish, I was studying Góngora and the "conceptista" poets of the seventeenth century, who liked to make connections between words, and also between concepts, and yoked these associations together to produce a most startling poetry. These poets were entranced by contrasts (dark/light, day/night, madness/sanity, reality/illusion) and metamorphoses, and ornamentation of all kinds. Looking at the supposedly sober, dignified and classical Racine in this light was going to be fun. I worked hard at that essay and it was a good one. Alas, I was involved in Total Theatre, and couldn't give the Baroque the attention it deserved until much later.

AN INTERLUDE OF SADNESS

I have to admit to not being entirely true to Michael during the first half of my first term. I had a brief flirtation with an athlete called Hugh from New College, but that wasn't really serious, so that when we drifted apart (quite painlessly) after a couple of weeks, I consoled myself with the thought that at least Michael was coming up to see me. I tidied my room. I bought crumpets to toast by the gas fire. We were going to eat them from my pale blue plates. The Madras cotton bedspread was smooth and inviting. Everything was ready. When Michael arrived I was reminded all over again of how wonderful he was and how much I loved him. We had tea and crumpets. Then he had to go and meet someone somewhere else. I think she had been a friend of his sister's. He would not be long. He would meet me outside Hertford College at six p.m. At six o'clock (dark, cold, November) I was outside Hertford. I was still there, weeping, at eight, when it became clear to me he was not going to appear. I stumbled down Holywell to where Braham and David had their digs. They let me in, and were both very kind to me, making me cups of horrible coffee, and distracting me with *Hang* chat. At about eleven, I staggered back to St Hilda's over Magdalen Bridge and wept new tears on to my friends' shoulders and was given more hot drinks. By the next morning, I was back in the Kemp as usual, scoffing cinnamon toast, and telling everyone that Braham wasn't nearly as forbidding as he looked: he was really quite human.

From Michael there was not one word of explanation, then or later. I have never laid eyes on him from that day to this. A few years ago, someone told me that he was married and worked in advertising.

SCENES FROM *HANG*

From the day of the first rehearsal in October until May of the next year, *Hang* took over the lives of everyone involved with it. We put together the outlines of the show before the Christmas vacation, we stayed up in Oxford for a couple of weeks after the end of term, and we opened in February. The show was newsworthy. In those days all plays had to go before the Lord Chamberlain, who was the Censor, and anything that was thought too disturbing or too violent or too rude had to be cut. We had run into arguments with this gentleman, who wanted to ban several of the more gruesome scenes, such as the re-enacting of the Rosenbergs' execution. In the end, a compromise was reached. We could read an account of the execution, but not imitate the actions. The University authorities were also not best pleased by a poster showing Emrys grimacing in a noose, but the picture was reproduced often in the papers, under the heading "Proctors Ban Poster". London papers, even before we opened, had been to take our photographs. There's one of me in the *Daily Sketch*. I'm trying to look sexy as best I can, in fishnet tights and a tiny skirt. The caption reads: "Judge's daughter in anti-hanging play". The fact that my father was a judge at this time was very useful to the publicity department. The critics were there on the first night and the reviews were excellent, although I have never quite forgiven John Higgins of the *Financial Times* for calling me a "stocky brunette". He was actually praising me, saying nice things about my songs, but "stocky". I shudder still. When the run at Oxford was over, we went to the Royal Shakespeare Theatre at Stratford and played the show there for a week, coming back to Oxford each night on a coach. Then Michael Codron brought us to the West End for a short season at the Comedy Theatre. The critics went into ecstasies all over again. We were discussed on Radio Three. One of the numbers from the show was televised for an arts programme called "Late Night Line-Up" on BBC2. In 1965, capital punishment was abolished in this country. Nothing to do with us really, but nevertheless...

Those are the bare facts. What follows is a kaleidoscopic impression of those few months, during which so many things were happening.

*Oh, What a Lovely War!* was devised as a seaside follies. *Hang* very quickly became a circus in the first half. After the interval the scene was a condemned cell, and we went through the whole procedure of a hanging from start to finish, in a surrealistic and heightened way. There was a dream sequence, and a horrifying Punch and Judy scene, leading to the execution. Woody, who came trailing clouds of glory from past prowess as a magician and bingo caller, was

a natural red-nosed clown. His yellow hair seemed
ready-made to be backcombed into a fuzzy aureole,
his Puckish face specifically designed for clown
make-up, and he had the energy and fizz of a Catherine wheel. Terry, who spoke through his nose, and
looked mournful even at his most hilarious, was the
perfect white-faced clown, and soon became the
embodiment of the Hanged Man. Jo and Emrys were
Ringmasters, Dick the Strong Man, and Bob the big,
bumbling, lovable clown, always a step behind the
others. No one quite expected his powerful rendition
of the song "Sam Hall", which shook the rafters at
every performance. The rest of us were jugglers and
bareback riders. Those of us ladies who added lustre
to a spangled leotard and tights (Jasmina, Hope, Viv
and Jane and Juliet but not me or Susan) ended up
as trapeze artists.

"The first shock lasted fifty-seven seconds," David
read from the account of the execution of the
Rosenbergs. We all stood motionless while Braham
timed us with a stopwatch. Fifty-seven seconds is
very long indeed when nothing but death is happening in it.

We ladies in our fishnets and high heels became a
chorus line for a song about Dartmoor, written by
Woody. He sang the jaunty little ditty so that it
dripped with the tawdry razzmatazz of a cheap
music hall, and we were kicking our legs in the air
behind him... "Tits and teeth!" Braham used to
growl. "Smile!" So we grinned away, and David
sang.

*Between you and the screw*
*There's a feeling that is new.*
*He's a friend both true and tried.*
*They've got more on the Moor than*
*they've ever had before,*
*And it's oh, so nice inside!*

Woody's talent for writing catchy tunes and lyrics
to match was a bonus. From his pen came the song
that drove home the physical nitty-gritty of a
hanging.

*One hundred and twelve, that's the magic*
*number*
*Divided by the weight of the body in stones.*
*You work it out and then you've got*
*The length of drop in feet.*
*Three cheers for Hangman Berry,*
*His system never can be beat!*

The music for *Hang* was a combination of existing
songs and others written by Woody and Iwan. The
fact that a person can make marks on paper that
then become beautiful sounds has never failed to
astonish me. One morning I went to fetch Iwan from
his room in Wadham on my way from College to the
rehearsal room in North Oxford. Iwan was bad at
waking up. I made him a cup of coffee and sat in his
study while he crashed about in his tiny bedroom,
getting dressed in a hurry. Braham was sure to look
even more cross and sad than usual if anyone was
late. Iwan was a big man with hunched shoulders
and long arms. He had permanent dark rings under

his eyes. He'd been to school in Liverpool, in the same class as Paul McCartney, and spoke with a soft Scouse accent. There was nothing he couldn't do with a piano and orchestra.

"Bloody hell," he said, lumbering into the study, unshaven. "Braham's going to kill me. I still haven't done that song ... hold on a sec."

He leaned on his desk, holding the lukewarm remains of his coffee in one hand and scribbling on the back of an envelope with the other. After about five minutes he said, "Right then, let's go," and we left. At the rehearsal room, he popped the envelope on the piano and played us, for the first time, the music he had written for "The Coiner's Lament". It was melancholy, poignant and lovely: one of those tunes that makes tears gather in the eyes and goose-flesh rise on the arms. Terry singing:

> *They all against the tripeman cry*
> *For coining he deserves to die...*

in his gloomy, nasal voice became one of the highlights of the show. Many people found it hard to believe that the melody was not a traditional one, like "Early One Morning".

Braham had all sorts of bright ideas for publicity. One of them was a breakfast party in full evening dress. We all trooped up the High and began to drink champagne with our bacon and eggs in a rather grotty café whose name has gone out of my head. We carried on, all of us, like something out of *Brideshead Revisited*. With hindsight, I suppose we

must have looked like a right load of twits, but at the
time I saw nothing wrong with it all. We paraded
along, in our floor-length dresses and dinner jackets,
talking and laughing at the tops of our voices, and I
suspect my voice was the loudest of all. Still, we got
into the newspaper.

Braham forbade me to listen to Billie Holiday singing
"Strange Fruit" because he didn't want me to try and
sound like her. The song was written especially for
her. It is bitter and harsh and full of anguish and
pain. After *Hang* was over I heard her searing version of it and was glad of Braham's prohibition. It
would have silenced me altogether. My other solo was
called "Geordie". I knew how Joan Baez sang it, but
tried to ignore what I'd heard. The two songs are
very moving. They were placed in the show at
moments where they contrasted with the noise and
colour and fun of the ensemble numbers. The aim of
*Hang* was to sway the audience and convince them
of the horrors of capital punishment, and Braham
and David used everything in their power to this end:
humour, spectacle, sentiment, lashings of music both
strident and sad, and statistics made real. All the way
through the show, we played small snatches of tape-
recorded voices, giving their views on hanging. And
all the way through, statements were read aloud,
which made the blood run cold, like this one from
Professor Joad, a man who used to appear regularly
on the radio programme called *The Brains Trust*,
"The objection to the death penalty is a piece of
canting sentimentality arising, I suppose, from the
doctrine that human life is sacred and should not be

taken." There was a song about Jack Ketch, who "loved to string the robbers up at Tyburn" which went with a swing, and one called "Gas!" with a cheery little chorus which went:

*On dilute sulphuric acid falls*
*Solid cyanide in cute little balls...*
*Gimme gas!*

# LOVE AND THE LONDON RUN

Before Christmas, I started going out with Richard. Richard was a show-off, like me. He'd *loved* the breakfast party, and gladly dressed up as Chopin to my Georges Sand for a Fancy Dress Party given by Hope. This occasion was special, not only because it was held in a Proper House and not a College, but also because, even after twenty-seven years, I remember the food: rice dishes studded with jewel-coloured vegetables, over-lapping slices of chicken and ham and beef, and vol-au-vents that created little explosions of pleasure in your mouth. It was quite unknown for a staircase party to yield more than a desultory crisp or a saucer of peanuts gritty with too much salt.

Richard was blond, with a big beaky nose. He actually *did* have a Chopin-ish look about him. I thought he was very Romantic. He liked poetry and was always discussing suicide. I was half impressed by him and half aware that he was not frightfully interesting under all that glittering surface. Gradually, as *Hang* took up more and more time, I saw less and less of him. He took me to the Varsity Rugby match at Twickenham to watch Oxford beat (or be beaten by) Cambridge. I can't remember who won. I didn't care at the time. I've never been so cold in all my life, even though Richard brought a rug and a flask of whisky. I think that was the end of our relationship.

For a while after that I went around with Iwan. I liked him enormously. I admired him. Not only was he amazingly gifted, he was also very funny. He arranged songs for me to sing in cabarets and smokers. Smokers were a kind of glorified party where comedians could try out their sketches and singers could test their songs in front of a friendly audience before exposing themselves on a public stage. Iwan liked my voice. He liked me. Long after I stopped going out with him, he remained a friend. I even did a charity show at Nottingham Playhouse for him after I was married and respectably teaching French in a girls' school in Manchester. We might have gone out for much longer if I hadn't fallen head over heels in love with Tim, who was the lighting designer on *Hang*.

Love! What a magical transformer it is! Girls who can't tell one end of a football pitch from another suddenly develop an encyclopaedic knowledge of the League. Others who used to think Rover was a dog's name become all clued up about the insides of cars. Because of Tim I suddenly became fascinated with cables, lighting cues, gels, battens, follow-spots, dimmer switches, etc., etc. I even learned how to wire up cables to huge plugs. I was there with Tim at the Playhouse as the set for *Twelfth Night* was struck, and the *Hang* company moved in to fit up ... oh, I learned all the necessary jargon! Tim was there all through the night, and so was I, fitting up like mad: one of the lads, dazzled and mesmerized by Tim's slender hips and air of nonchalant technical brilliance. I'm still, after all this time, very attentive to lighting changes in any play I go and see.

A dark, skinny, shy, bespectacled young man called John, who was actually reading Music, set the rules of the Bodleian Library (which all prospective readers had to recite) as an operatic aria for Bob to sing at an OUDS smoker. This brought the house down. At about the same time, perhaps even for the same smoker, John set a lyric of mine to music. It was the only song I've ever written, all about a cellist falling in love with a second violinist. He turned it into fake Schubert. The words weren't up to much but the tune was terrific. I still sometimes hum it as I peel the potatoes, hearing the piano in my mind: all those watery arpeggios running up and down in the left hand.

Viv was a witch. A white witch, she hastened to tell us. She had hennaed hair and a bird-like face. She was also a very brilliant scholar and knew all there was to know about *Tristan and Iseult*. She was both matter-of-fact and fanciful. During the London run of *Hang* many of the company, including Viv, stayed in a very big house in Chester Square belonging to the then Chancellor of the Exchequer, who was, of course, conveniently ensconced in No. 11 Downing Street.*

*Yes, his son at Merton knew the Company Manager who knew ... who knew... Connections of this kind are always part of Oxford life and have ever given its denizens many unfair advantages. If you look at any branch of the arts or politics or business, you can find lots of people who were at Oxford and Cambridge together and this creates a sort of network of people who knew each other well when they were young and who feel a certain loyalty to those whom they remember from their youth. This network has very obvious advantages, and is one of the reasons that it's often seen as an exclusive club which is a little chilly towards outsiders.

Viv was for ever seeing blokes in eighteenth-century gear appearing behind her head in the dressing-table mirror as she applied positively Egyptian black lines to her eyelids. Once I went to see her at her digs, and as I was leaving, she called out, "Some people have noticed a Presence on the first landing, so do be careful!"

She always dressed in special robes for her rituals at solstice time, Walpurgisnacht and so forth, but had given up reading palms.

"I've seen too much," she would mutter darkly into frothy coffee at the Kemp, staring at us from under lowered lashes.

When we were performing at the Playhouse, we took to haunting the Playhouse Bar. We didn't desert the Kemp ... after all, the Playhouse served no anchovy toast or buttered teacakes. Still, we moved to the Playhouse, once we'd eaten, more and more frequently.

The first week of the London run coincided with my Preliminary Exams. Not sitting them was out of the question. Not being in *Hang* was unthinkable. Therefore, I would have to do both. Discussions were held at the highest level, and a plan was devised. I would do my exams, morning and afternoon, dressed in subfusc, of course. Then, when I'd finished, I'd run down the steps and into a car belonging to a very nice medical student called John. He would then drive to London, arriving in time for us to snatch something to eat before the show. I then did the show, and at the end of the performance, if

I was quick putting my subfusc back on, there was just time for a speedy drink at the pub with the others before leaping into the car and driving through the dark, back to Oxford. On these journeys, I often imagined a soundtrack of the kind of desperate music used to indicate car chases on silent films. Once we'd arrived at St Hilda's, I had to climb in. The place where this was done was a small gate. Roses had been sadistically trained to grow up the iron railings. I am a person who never managed to jump over anything in gym (not the horse, not the box: nothing) and now suddenly I was required to clamber over railings, running a serious risk of impaling myself, tearing my clothes, totally destroying my tights and, worst of all, getting caught. I did it for four nights, clambering into Wendy's window and then falling quite exhausted into bed. Two exams and a show in one day was more than a body could take. Every white shirt I put on ended the day with orangey Leichner grease-paint all around the collar.

It goes without saying that I failed my Prelims. I was summoned and told off severely. I was the first scholar in the entire history of St Hilda's who hadn't managed to pass Prelims. They didn't take my scholarship away, for which I was grateful. No, they were magnanimous and let me sit the exam again, but they did ban me from acting in the summer term. (Before appearing in any production, you had to get Acting Permission from your tutor. This was obviously withheld if your work was seen to be suffering.) So, I was unable to be Lady Bracknell in *The Importance of Being Earnest* – a part I had been thrilled to get, and was longing to do. I'd been perfecting an interpretation based on one of my art teachers at school which would have been ... never mind. Such dreams evaporated rapidly under the regretful glances of my teachers. They had obviously failed to grasp just how total Total Theatre could be.

The London run went to my head. The West End... We were professionals. We were Stars. We arrived at the theatre and said "Hello" to George at the Stage Door. We had dressing rooms with light bulbs round the mirrors. Princess Margaret was photographed by the Press coming to see the show. I walked round Leicester Square thinking: I wonder if anyone recognizes me? Will someone stop me and ask for an autograph? No one did. I put it down to the fact that I took my glasses off to appear on stage and no one spotted me as being the same person when I had them on.

My father had by this time been sent to Guyana (taking the Map of Oxford with him), but my mother had a field day while *Hang* was on, sniffing out every word about us that was printed in every newspaper or magazine, however obscure. She had taken a little flat for the duration of the London run. I was with Tim most of the time, either at his flat, or wandering round London, or even on a few occasions in the launderette with him, blissfully watching his clothes go round and round in the sudsy water. Still, my mother wasn't lonely. A lot of relatives came from all over the place to see the show: my Aunt Vivienne from Cardiff, my Aunt Sara (who was a

travel agent and got cheap tickets) from Israel and
my Aunt Dina from New York. After Dina had been
to see *Hang* she spent many happy hours trawling
the shoe shops looking for pink shoes.

"There must be pink shoes in New York," I said,
but London in 1964 was already showing signs of
turning into a swinging city, and pink shoes of a
highly trendy variety were a distinct possibility.

Dick spent the early part of 1964 singing "I Want
to Hold Your Hand" by the Beatles. He sang it
all the time, and so did the rest of us. It became a
kind of theme song for those days. We all did an
awful lot of giggling. Once, as we were waiting in
the wings to go on stage for the calypso number,
Dick said to me: "It's funny, isn't it, Addle? ... Sex.
I mean, if you think about it... It's amazing more
people don't just burst out laughing when they're
right in the middle ... or maybe they do, and no one
says anything ... I mean, if you really stop and
think about it..."

People were for ever trying to make one another
laugh on stage. It's called "corpsing". As I was without my glasses, I could never catch anyone's eye, or
get the giggles when a particularly silly expression
appeared on someone's face.

Once, after a lunchtime twenty-first birthday party
at which the champagne had been rather plentiful,
almost the entire company arrived tipsy at the
theatre for the matinée. We tottered through the
opening number, the circus parade and calypso, and
then when we came off, Braham's voice at its cross-

est came over the tannoy: "That was the most unprofessional display I've ever seen in my life, and if you don't immediately sober up, I shall personally bring down the curtain."

We all sobered up at once. The show must go on.

*   *   *

The edge of the stage at the Comedy Theatre went down in steps to the stalls. During the Dartmoor song one night, as we high-stepped and kicked our way downstage in the chorus-girl routine, I took one stride too many (oh, it's a dreadful risk, going on stage almost unable to see!) and found myself walking down the steps. The chorus line ground relentlessly on, grinning away (tits and teeth) and I was left to chase after them and catch them up. Perhaps, I thought, if I'm ridiculous enough, they'll think it's a deliberate attempt to be funny.

I suppose there must have been parties to mark the end of *Hang* in London. I don't remember them. I date the end of the show more accurately as 30 April, 1964. This was the eve of my first May Morning. May Morning figures strongly in Oxford mythology. One is supposed to dance all night and watch the dawn rise over Magdalen College while listening to madrigals sung high up in the tower by choirboys with golden voices. That's the tradition. I was looking forward to it with anticipation, excitement, longing, even glee. It would be perfect. Tim had invited me to a dance. We would be together the whole night and the music would play and at last we would walk with our arms around each other to Magdalen and watch the mauve daybreak and feel our hearts rise like the sweet notes of the choirboys... Oh, it would be idyllic.*

I made my way to Tim's room in Merton College, as arranged. There, before even offering me a drink, and in the nicest and most gentlemanly way possible (He had a lovely quiet voice and beautiful manners. That was one of the things I liked about him. He was so elegant.) Tim said he didn't think we should go out together any more. When words like that come at you through the air, however pleasantly spoken and kindly expressed, you lose all your intelligence. The sensible questions like:

1) When exactly did you stop loving me? You were quite normal yesterday.

2) Why?

3) What have I done?

4) Is there anyone else? (There wasn't.)

5) Why *now*? Couldn't it have waited till after May Morning? Did you *have* to spoil that?

all go out of your head and you want to curl up under a quilt somewhere and howl for days and days. I managed to say nothing at all (a great achievement for me) and not to let one single tear fall until I was right outside Merton. What was I supposed to do now? Everyone else was at parties of their own. There would be no one in college to cheer me up. Should I go to some other gathering and be a (rather chubby) skeleton at the feast? In the end, I sat all night on a bench near the Botanical Gardens and opposite Magdalen, weeping on and off, and looking at all the other revellers as they passed by. I'm

---

*There was another, less romantic celebration of spring around at this time: "Hurray, hurray, the first of May. Outdoor sex begins today."

damned (I thought to myself) if Tim is going to make me miss my first May Morning. I was terribly angry with him. I was sad. I still loved him (although that was beginning to dwindle a little under the force of the anger). I had been cheated of a treat, my eyes were puffy and red, and yet part of me, a tiny part of me was there on the outside, watching and thinking: this'd make a good story ... abandoned by boyfriend ... crying all night ... fade into heartbreakingly beautiful music floating from the tower as dawn streaks the sky with pink. I could almost see it on the screen. It was a kind of consolation. And *Hang* was over.

# BACK TO
# NORMAL

**F**ood is of tremendous importance in my life.
I apologize to anyone who is bored by the
subject and advise them to skip this section
altogether. Food has always preoccupied me. I am
greedy – that's the truth. At boarding-school food
was mostly disgusting, but those few treats we did
have (fruit crumbles, baked beans on fried bread,
rolls and honey on a Sunday morning) kept us going.
Food was a subject for discussion, second only to
Boys. If your parents took you out for the day, you
had to give your friends a mouthful-by-mouthful
description when you returned.

At Oxford we spent a lot of time deciding where
to eat. Roaming about in gangs of about twenty or
so, we would descend on the Fantasia (Italian-ish) or
one of the Chinese restaurants, or the Taj, the
Cobra, the Himalaya ("Eat dirt cheap at the
Himalaya" – that was the slogan) or the Dildunia,
which was my favourite place to go for Indian food.
It had wonderful scarlet flocked wallpaper, and was
very near the Scala cinema.

Once we'd all settled around a whole lot of

pushed-together tables, we started ordering. This took ages. If you were lucky enough to have someone present with a piece of paper and a pencil about their person, then they might write down the order. Otherwise the scene quickly began to resemble the crowded-cabin sequence from *A Night at the Opera*, where Groucho Marx keeps ordering more and more food: "Make that three hard-boiled eggs!"

If ordering was chaos, paying was even worse. The bill had to be meticulously divided by the number of people, and then piteous cries would rend the air,

"I only had one poppadam!"

"Have you charged me for a pudding?"

"I ordered a paratha..."

"No, I did not have two Cokes..." etc., etc.

Pennies, shillings, bits and pieces of this and that filled the saucer. Then we'd have a whip round for the tip. By the time the process was over, we were all hungry again.

College food, apart from breakfast, was tasteless. There was even a protest about it once. A whole delegation of St Hilda's students actually met the catering staff. I suggested that some garlic scattered about the casseroles and savoury dishes would improve matters, but this helpful culinary hint was mocked, scorned and snubbed by the cooks. The food continued as bland and gloppy as before. I'm sure it's now much better. Institutions undergo a one hundred per cent improvement the minute I leave them. Young women at St Hilda's now have keys to come in after midnight and are allowed to bring young men into College for the weekend!

Back to food... Posher meals were taken at the

Capri, the Cantina or the Sorbonne, and *extremely* posh meals, which were also desperately expensive, were to be had at the Elizabeth, just a hop, skip and a jump away from Pembroke. Anyone who took you to the Elizabeth was (a) Rich (b) Serious About You or (c) Both. I still wake up in the night sometimes yearning for their Crème Brulée. The first time I had it, I was so overcome, I ordered another one straight away. In my three years at Oxford, I went to the Elizabeth only three times. I did, however, become an expert on Scotch eggs, chicken-and-mushroom pies and pub notions of mixed salads.

MOVIES
The movies are a pleasure which adds not one gram to your weight, nor one centimetre to your hips, if you can eschew the popcorn, choc-ices and rubbery hot-dogs. I have been a movie addict since my early (pre-television) childhood. In Borneo, when I was eight, I used to sit with my friend Monica in the Circle at least three times a week, watching such wonders as *Pagan Love Song* starring Esther Williams and Howard Keel, or the latest Jane Powell hit. At school, movies we were shown tended towards the improving: lives of Queen Victoria or Florence Nightingale or, if we were lucky, comedies like *Kind Hearts and Coronets* or *The Lavender Hill Mob*. Every time I went out with my parents for the day, we would go to the pictures. I loved Westerns. I loved Musicals. I loved Comedies. I loved Courtroom Dramas. I loved Historical Romances. I loved Thrillers. There was very little I didn't love. If it moved, that was good enough for me.

At Oxford, I discovered the French New Wave, Orson Welles, Eisenstein, Bergman, Fellini, etc. The film that made the strongest impact was *Jules et Jim* by François Truffaut. It's a wonderfully poignant and romantic story of a woman who is loved by two friends, and who loves each of them in a different way. It also has the most glorious music running through it. I went back to see it four times during the week it was on. I have seen it a few times on TV since then and I still love it. Jeanne Moreau is who I wish I looked like, and I still sing the song (wonderful round-and-round music, like a fairground carousel, and wistful, slightly world-weary lyrics) in my bathroom and kitchen.

CLOTHES

Fashionwise, it was a time when I should probably have gone into hiding. The Mini was upon us, and I ought to have shunned it, but I didn't. I wore short skirts and dark tights and sometimes white tights, although I never went as far as white plastic boots. Everybody was very Body Conscious in those days, and the bodies they were conscious of looked like Twiggy and Jean Shrimpton. Therefore I always felt myself to be fat, even though actually I was probably no more than plump. This plumpness was (is) not helped by a lack of height and a distressing shortness of leg. However, none of this has ever prevented me from trying to follow the fashion, and from loving clothes and jewels and dressing up in any way I can.

This was also the era of the High Heeled Shoe. I cannot emphasize too strongly the liberation that

Flat Shoes (the blessed Trainer and the glorious Doc Marten) brought us. I think my feet must have been hurting for a major proportion of my youth. I also wore various shapes of trousers, although these were always black because black was supposed to be slimming. All my jumpers, blouses, etc., hung loosely over my hips on the "hiding a multitude of sins" principle. Laura Ashley opened a shop in Oxford in my last year and transformed me into a buxom Victorian wench.

I remember several outfits in detail.

1) A fuschia-pink smock-type dress, ending three inches or so above the knee.

2) A wonderful full-length jungle-print evening dress made by Franny in about two hours. It had no sleeves, and sort of gathered itself round my neck on a drawstring, leaving my shoulders bare. (NB to plump young women: do not despair. Your waist may not be up to much, but your shoulders, neck and cleavage will be terrific!)

3) A bottle-green knitted dress from Marks and Spencer, like a very long jumper. I thought I might end up looking elegant like Liz, but discovered quickly that knitted dresses cling to one's bottom with dismaying tenacity.

4) A bright scarlet duffel-type jacket which I loved and wish I still had.

5) A black dress I used to sing in whenever I did cabaret. Everything they say about little black dresses is true.

6) My first Laura Ashley: a full-skirted, cap-sleeved pinafore in blue cotton printed with white swans.

Apart from my own clothes, I also have a good memory for other people's.

1) An orange wool pinafore dress with a square neck worn by Dick's girlfriend during the *Hang* period, Lynn of the Never-ending Legs.*

2) Nancy's black leather subfusc skirt. But then, she was American.

3) Marina's black pin-striped trouser suit worn with a black and white checked shirt.†

4) Franny in an assortment of 1920s-style glittery, shimmery things, usually picked up in the market.

5) My future husband in a rust-coloured hand-knitted jumper that was worn till it fell to pieces ten years later.

And so on...

VINCE – BEING A COUPLE

The great advantage of writing fiction is that you can invent. If you feel you need speed, excitement, pace, emotion, etc., you can order your narrative in such a way that these elements can appear at the appointed time. If you have to be truthful, then the whole enterprise can turn into a catalogue: I went out with this person, then that person, then that one, I appeared in this play, then that play, then that one, and so forth. But I went out with Vince for over a year, so I have to write about that time, and about him.

Vince was at Pembroke, reading PPE (Philosophy,

---

*Lynn was one of the few people who was built for the mini. I used to gaze at her knees with severe pangs of envy.

†This impressed me so much, I put it in a story called "Snapshots of Paradise". (In *Daydreams on Video* published by Lightning Books.)

Politics and Economics). Gosh, I thought when I
first met him: Pembroke! My father's college!
There's something Significant about that, surely?
I knew who he was before I met him. He was a
director of plays. I'd seen his excellent production of
Pinter's *The Birthday Party*. He came sometimes,
though not often, to the Kemp or the Playhouse Bar.
Shortly after the May Morning fiasco with Tim,
I went to hear Joan Littlewood speak one evening at
Univ. as a guest of the ETC. After her talk, a whole
gang of us went for a meal at the Cantina. The
talking went on and on, long after midnight. I was
sitting next to Vince. He was interesting. He was
attractive. He wasn't very tall, but he did have wavy
black hair and extremely blue eyes. I can't remember anything we said, but I do recall him walking me
back to St Hilda's through the deserted streets.
It must have been nearly morning. The grey and
golden towers stood out against a sky of palest green.
When I was very young, I used to make ornate
decorations for sand-castles by grabbing a handful of
sloppy sand and dribbling it slowly out of my
clenched fist. The tiny droplets formed themselves
into entrancingly precarious peaks and spires, and
that was what the buildings looked like that morning. Vince kissed me in the shadow of the wall that
ran along the side of St Hilda's. At about eleven
forty-five every night, you could see dozens of cou-
ples having a last smooch before the gates
(metaphorically) clanged shut. I'd vowed I'd never
line up like that, but there was no one about at this
hour. I flew over the gate like a bird, buoyed up by
the beginnings of a New Love. That was what it felt

like. To anyone watching, it was probably the same
old struggle with Railings and Roses.

Vince and I quickly became a Couple. This had
advantages and disadvantages. Of course, as I was in
love, I saw only the advantages. These were:

1) You always had someone around – to eat meals
with, to go to parties with, give tea to, be with all the
time. You were never lonely. You were hardly ever
alone.

2) You acquired an extra slice of life by immediately meeting all your boyfriend's other friends, the
ones you did not have in common. My future husband was one of these.

3) You gained status. You were someone whom
someone else liked enough to go about with all the
time. If your boyfriend was A Director, you shared
some of his reflected glory. If you had any glory of
your own (and to be truthful, those of us who had
been in *Hang* did consider ourselves slightly more
glorious than everyone else) then that reflected on
him.

4) The pressure of having to Find True Love, or
even Untrue Love, at a staircase party was off. You
could relax and enjoy yourself.

The disadvantages were:

1) Staircase parties ceased to be an adventure, and
became a bit of a drag. Not only could you not talk
to anyone properly, you also had to keep a weather
eye open to make sure your Other Half was not
treading the primrose path of dalliance with some

dewy-complexioned Fresher.

2) *You* could not tread the said primrose path, etc., etc.

3) You saw an awful lot less of your girlfriends.

4) You saw an awful lot less of your textbooks.

5) You risked life and limb not only climbing into St Hilda's but climbing *out* of Pembroke – a fiendishly difficult operation which took the combined efforts of Vince and a few of his friends on more than one occasion.

CLICHÉS

Hearty young men with ostentatious incomes and no chins to speak of, Commemoration Balls, punts on the river: Oxford has collected to itself so many clichéd images that it now positively begs not to be written about. When I first arrived there, I was quite ready to immerse myself in all this *Brideshead*-ery, but soon discovered that these images were less desirable than they looked. Take the rich young men. I met very few of them, and they were either uninterested in my charms or I was uninterested in theirs. Most people I liked came from ordinary homes: Iwan's parents lived in a small semi in a Liverpool suburb, and Vince's had exactly the same kind of house in Cheltenham. There were, alas, no grand house parties à la Evelyn Waugh for me during the vacations. I did once persuade a pleasant young man called Jeremy to take me to a Young Conservatives Ball which was being held at Blenheim Palace, because I wanted that particular movie-in-the-head: me waltzing with a scion of the aristocracy at Blenheim. Once I'd got over my excitement at the splendour of the surroundings, I spent the evening hovering round the buffet table, avoiding Young Conservatives.

Punting on the river was definitely part of the Oxford myth. Through the winter months I had frequently pictured myself garbed in floaty chiffon and wearing a straw hat heavy with pink roses, being punted along on a perfect day by someone who was both divinely handsome and totally devoted to me, through hanging willow branches and beside jewelled meadows. A picnic came into this dream, and so did whispers from onlookers on the bank to the effect of: "Who is that fascinating creature?" Alas, the reality fell short, as reality often does. By the time summer came, I was going out with Vince who was quite bored by the river and all its works. I also discovered that when you *did* decide to get a punt, you had to wait ages till one was free, pay money that you could ill afford, and then negotiate your way upstream or downstream through scores of other punts, playing a kind of water-dodgems. Then other friends wanted to come too, so you were all squashed up, the air was filled with midges, and there was *always* a thin film of greenish liquid at the bottom of the punt, so wasn't it lucky you had chosen the filthy jeans and not the floaty chiffon?

I only went to two balls (as opposed to mere parties) during my three years. The first was the aforementioned Blenheim affair, and the other was the Pembroke Ball, to which Vince invited me in the first flush of New Romance. I decided very quickly that these occasions were a complete waste of time and money for the following reasons:

1) The weather was *never* hot enough for the kind of clothes you had to wear: long, very strapless dresses. Even with a shawl, I was shivering by ten o'clock. A nice fluffy cardy would have done the trick, but you can't wear one with a Posh Frock. You also had to do a lot of teetering on lawns in stiletto heels.

2) The places where you were supposed to dance were always packed.

3) You could never get enough to eat to justify the exorbitant price of the tickets.

4) You spent ages aimlessly trailing around looking for things to do and people to talk to, but more often than not, your sensible friends had stayed away and were probably at this very moment feasting on Chicken Biryani after a good double bill at the Scala.

5) You weren't allowed to go home till you'd had breakfast at about five in the morning, so you were exhausted and your feet were killing you.

In spite of all this, people flocked to the Commems. Some daring folk (a friend of mine called Howard excelled at this) made a point of never paying, but gatecrashing every possible occasion, which at least added an element of danger to the proceedings. Sometimes famous bands came to play: the Rolling Stones, just started and newly popular, were at Magdalen in 1965 or '66, but we stayed away and listened to their records instead. At least the Pembroke Ball was in Pembroke, so Vince and I spent most of the time in his room, drinking comforting cups of coffee in the warmth, while outside his windows we could hear the excited squeals of revellers drinking champagne (that closely resembled Lucozade) in a howling gale.

MAY MORNING 1965

If my first May Morning was sentimental and weepy,
my second resembled one of those irritating and pretentious movies where all sorts of beautiful images
chase one another across the screen without anyone
quite understanding what's going on. By May 1965,
I'd been going out with Vince for nearly a year. I
don't think we had any special plans to celebrate
May Morning – that was the kind of thing First
Years did. We were sitting in the King's Arms and
suddenly there were four young men chatting to us
whom we'd never laid eyes on before. They were (see
Pretentious Movies, above) wearing evening dress. It
turned out that they were a string quartet ... yes,
there were the instruments, all around their feet and
leaning against the wall. They had to kill time.
They'd been hired by a Rich Young Man, probably
at Christ Church, to play quartets at a dawn party.
Going to bed and setting their alarms for later on did
not, naturally, cross their minds. No, they would
wassail the night away and stagger to their gig as
best they could. Then someone (it might have been
Pete: he built a lot of sets and was a good friend of
Vince's) came in in a panic. The cherry trees flat for
*The Cherry Orchard* had to be repainted by the next
day ... all the blossom looked like used cotton wool.
We trooped off through the night and the musicians
came too. All through the hours of darkness, in
something that looked like a furniture warehouse
somewhere far beyond Pembroke, we painted and
painted till our arms were aching. Old sofas loomed
out of the shadows. The floor echoed when we
walked on it, and through the night the four musi-

cians played. The melodies of Mozart and Schubert
and Brahms poured out and filled the cavernous
spaces, moved in the dust and hovered in the corners, draped themselves over the armchairs and
hung in the light of unshaded bulbs. Just before
dawn, the quartet left. We never saw any of them
again. We were all exhausted, but the cherry tree flat
was painted to Pete's satisfaction. I remember thinking: shall I go and sit on Magdalen Bridge again?
Listen to the voices on the silvery air? The lumpy
sofa I'd subsided on to suddenly seemed as inviting
as a feather bed. I curled up as best I could and fell
asleep for a few hours.

MAY MORNING 1966
I was quite blasé about Oxford Tradition by this
time, and was also (at last) working for my final
exams. I did some work, and then went to sleep in
my own room in College and didn't wake up till
breakfast time.

WEATHER
Endless days of golden summer, opalescent days of
equally golden autumn, crisply-bracing bright blue
days of sparkling winter: that's the kind of weather
you generally find as the backdrop to both fiction
and autobiography. When it comes to fiction, I'm a
great believer in golden/opalescent/sparkling, etc.,
myself. If, however, we are dealing with any kind of
truth here, I have to say (and you won't find many
autobiographers admitting as much: the days of
one's youth are supposed to be surrounded by an
aureole of Goldenness) that the weather in Oxford

was frequently wet, dull, grey, chilly, freezing, miserable and dank. It was weather as we all know it to be in the UK in real life. Oxford is just as lovely in the rain as it is in the sunshine, but naturally you're less in the mood to appreciate its glories with a damp gown flapping round your ankles and your whole face bunched up into a grimace around your nose to avoid the wind.

# OUTDOOR PRODUCTIONS

*A MIDSUMMER NIGHT'S DREAM* AND
*ALICE IN WONDERLAND*

From May onwards, a rash of summer productions would break out all over Oxford. It stood
to reason. There were so many tempting
gardens (Worcester, Merton, Christ Church, Trinity,
etc.) whose greensward, lovingly tended over cen-
turies, was simply crying out for Shakespeare and
other classics to be declaimed all over it by young
people in ill-fitting tights and full-length dresses.
Oxford terms are only eight weeks long, therefore
this al fresco cavorting would extend into the
summer vacation. I feel about outdoor productions
roughly the same as I do about picnics: they're a
positive idyll when everything is perfect and a pain
when the weather decides to be difficult. On the
whole, I can't see any good reason not to a) eat at a
table in a nice, warm house or b) act in a theatre
complete with loos and dressing rooms. Still, I do
have to admit that the two outdoor shows I was in
did have the most spectacular settings.

In July 1964, Vince directed *A Midsummer
Night's Dream* in the grounds of the Alveston

Manor Hotel at Stratford. According to the local paper at the time, this was the precise spot of "The Dream's" first production four hundred years before. I don't know how they found that out, nor whether it's true, but it made a good headline. I was given the part of Flute, the bellows-mender, only, I fear, because I was the director's girlfriend. Still, I cut my hair boyishly short and reasoned that even in Elizabethan times, there must have been a few tubby little bellows-menders walking about. I also (because the part of Flute is not exactly taxing) doubled as a kind of minstrel-ess, wandering around among the audience before the play started, wrapped in a cloak with the hood pulled well up, singing away at the top of my voice. This was supposed to induce Elizabethan twinges in everyone's breast as they sat down to watch the fun. We didn't know many songs of that period, so it was "Greensleeves" and "Waley Waley" and dear old "Geordie" from *Hang*, which wasn't really the right century, but had a plaintive olde-worldiness about it. The play worked beautifully. Woody was Puck to perfection, Bob was an endearing Bottom, and Dick and Lynn towered over us in majestic splendour as Theseus and Hippolyta. Jenny from St Hilda's played Hermia, which was the part I'd hankered after, and with her looks (she resembled Theda Bara, the silent-movie actress) she smouldered through the lines, and I had to admit I was better suited to Flute.

The setting was very pretty: lawns and swelling banks whereon the wild thyme might quite probably be seen growing, and a gigantic cedar tree to play about with. The progress of the court of Athens over the grass to the performing area was magnificent to behold, but we had to listen very carefully for cues. The exits and entrances were yards and yards away from the acting area. It often took a full minute to arrive onstage. Perhaps for this reason, Vince decided we all needed to do exercises before each rehearsal. "Warming-up" he called it, years before anyone knew what aerobics were.

"Bloody Nazi!" muttered Dick every morning as he creaked, bad-temperedly into action. "Bloody exercises!" A lot of snorting and moaning followed.

The Alveston Manor Hotel looked luxurious, but we were all living in caravans round the back where the residents couldn't see us. These caravans were small, hot, uncomfortable and induced a mild claustrophobia in most of us by the time we left them. Franny met an actor from the Royal Shakespeare Company and went out with him for one evening. That caused a bit of excitement. We all sat in the pub near the Theatre, trying to spot famous people. I think I saw the actor David Warner at the bar, but it was hard to be sure. There were quite a lot of tall, cadaverous-looking men about in those days in the purlieus of the RSC.

1965 was the centenary of the first publication of *Alice's Adventures in Wonderland* by Lewis Carroll, a book which can claim to be one of the most Oxford-y works ever written. Adrian (an eccentric Divinity student who had already produced a wild and wonderful *Hunting of the Snark* for one night only in the Holywell Music Rooms) hit upon the idea of an outdoor "Alice" set in Christ Church Meadow. The original Alice was one of the daughters of Dean

Liddell of Christ Church, and when the weather per-
mitted, we rehearsed in the Dean's garden: a place
generally speaking not open to the public. I couldn't
quite get over it. Not having very much to do at
rehearsals, I used to lie on the grass and watch the
others and say to myself: this is it. This is the *real*
Alice's *real* garden. She must have sat here with her
sisters. I'm not a believer in ghosts, but I did look
for Alice, because that small garden was an enchanted
place. What I had to do in the play was this: sit up
a tree on a specially designed platform and every
time someone on stage sang a song ("How Doth the
Little Crocodile", "You Are Old, Father William",
etc.) I had to sing the original Victorian hymn or
song that Carroll was sending up. I think I was supposed to be Alice's sister. All that could be seen of
me was the hem of my long skirt peeping through
the foliage. This was fortunate, because I didn't have
acting permission, and appeared in the programme
under a pseudonym. The reason for this was: I'd
used up my acting ration appearing as (*sic*) Zenobia
Bogus-Bogus in a musical called (*sic* again) *You
Can't Do Much Without a Screwdriver* of which
more later.

Tammy was Alice, and looked like a Tenniel illus-
tration come to life. The whole production was as
faithful as possible to those astonishing pictures,
Adrian reasoning (quite rightly, I think) that a
fat percentage of one's image of Alice comes from
Tenniel's pictures.

During the summer vacation, we took the production to the outdoor theatre at Minnack in Cornwall
and set it among the rocks and crags overlooking the

sea. Every night, in that amazingly beautiful place, I pitted my un-amplified voice against the waves of the Channel, which much of the time were obligingly whispery and quiet. Most of the company slept in a large church hall. All the sleeping bags lined up on the floor at night looked like rows and rows of butterflies in the larval stage of their development. Vince and I had a tent in the churchyard, and tents soon ousted caravans from their number one position at the top of the "Uncomfortable Habitation" chart. It rained unceasingly the first few days we were in Cornwall, and at night time, moisture seeped in under the ground sheet despite our best efforts.

*SOME MORE PEOPLE*

JANE
Jane designed the costumes for *A Midsummer Night's Dream*, and I spent all my time at Oxford admiring her from a distance. I can't say I knew her at all well, but she was everything I was not: painfully thin, elegant, eccentric in a way one associated with hostesses of the Edwardian era. She was a postgraduate, and lived in a house in North Oxford. This house was full of treasures, all jumbled up pellmell: feathers, stones, shells, beautiful china, pages covered in her wonderfully detailed drawings, cushions, shawls, lace, satin, bits of this and that and the other and all beautiful. Jane was enigmatic. She had a mysterious smile, and dark blue eyes and long lashes. Iwan was devoted to her, and so were many others. All sorts of fascinating people could be found in her house, drinking China tea.

LOUIE

Louie was my scout for two years. I never knew her surname. Scouts are college servants, who come in and clean your room for you. This was a relationship I found embarrassing. I didn't like the thought of a woman old enough to be my granny cleaning up my dirty ashtrays. I wasn't often in my room while she was there, but when I was, we chatted. She told me once that after her husband had been very ill, they'd changed places in bed, so that he could be near the door or away from the window, or both.

"I never slept a wink," Louie said. "Not for all that time. I just couldn't get used to the other side of the bed. Well, not after forty years, now could I?"

Scouts were people who could, if they felt like it, tell tales on you. Anyone staying out all night, either for a fit-up at the theatre, or anything else, had to arrange beforehand for a kind friend to go into her room and mess up the bed. Your Scout had to think you'd spent the night in college, or you could be in bad trouble.

ROBERT PRING-MILL

Because St Hilda's had no one teaching Spanish in the College, I was "farmed out" to Robert Pring-Mill (first of New College and later of St Catherine's). I went to tutorials at his house in Hamilton Road almost every week for three years and it was for him that I tried my hardest and did my best work. Partly this was because he was such a nice person: very gentle and softly spoken, with a twinkle in his eye and a smile in constant use. He looked like an older version of one of those heroes of 1950s war films, where the men were all good chaps together. What was even better, his wife often had tea and cakes just ready to be served as I arrived. He thought my essays were good, so we had a very happy relationship. It's wonderful how one's work blossoms when the teacher admires your efforts. Some of the pleasure I took in my Spanish tutorials, though, did come from what I was studying. I wallowed in the poetry of Góngora, Quevedo, Garcilaso de la Vega, the plays of Calderón and Lope de Vega and the prose of Cervantes. Before writing my essays, I would make a huge and elaborate plan on a gigantic piece of cartridge paper, full of dotted lines, arrows, circled notes, and jottings in every colour of ink I could find. I grew very attached to these plans. I kept them rolled up in my room and used them in my third year for revision purposes. It was much easier to look at a diagrammatic representation of an essay than to plough through twenty sides of prose. One night, I sat up all through the night, writing a saga about Góngora's "Polifemo". Someone gave me a couple of Benzedrine tablets* to keep me awake. They also made me feel high and the essay was longer than ever and positively fizzed along.

YOU CAN'T DO MUCH WITHOUT A SCREWDRIVER
This was a musical (words by Chris, music by John) directed by Woody. It had Bob as the Governor General of a mythical island called Amnesia. His name was Sir Somebody or Other Bogus-Bogus, and

---

*Please note these tablets. They are my one and only experience of Drugs. I must confess to never having taken so much as a single puff of a joint.

Susan was his Lady wife. Adrian played a butler
called Trousers which led to lines you could see
coming a mile off, like: "There are no flies on
trousers!" Diana and I were, respectively, Amanda
and Zenobia Bogus-Bogus, the Governor's daughters. There were two young heroes and two baddies
and the plot had something to do with blowing up
Government House. Diana and I had a wonderful
"suffragette" production number called "Emancipa-
tion", which went on for a full six minutes of
singing and dancing with the ladies' chorus. I liked
the costumes, which were vaguely Victorian, and for
once I appeared on stage looking halfway decent.
My real efforts at glamour, however, I reserved for
my cabaret dates.

CABARET
As well as revues which were put on at the Playhouse and had casts of thousands, I also did a few
cabaret performances of my own with Iwan at the
piano. The most prestigious was my appearance in
the Union Bar, dressed in black from head to foot,
and wearing sunglasses and white lipstick. I sang
"Twelve Gates to the City", "This Train" and a fair
sprinkling of Joan Baez songs: "All My Trials",
"East Virginia" and good old "El Preso Numero
Nueve". Barbra Streisand was just at the beginning
of her popularity. Maggie had one of her records,
and I persuaded Iwan into a version of "Super
market in Old Peking", which went at a fair old lick
and left us gasping for breath. I also sang (because
the Beach Boys and Dylan were our favourites)
Iwan's arrangements of "Don't Think Twice, It's

Alright" and "Sloop John B". I even sang "You
Make Me Feel So Young", which reminded me of
when I was going out with Tim.

Another cabaret I enjoyed doing was master-
minded by Jo and put on in (I think) Lady Margaret
Hall. This was an Edwardian occasion, and I sang
"The Piccadilly Johnny with the Little Glass Eye"
dressed in a man's evening suit.

One of the ETC revues exists on a record called
"Seven-a-Side" which I still have. We're all there on
the cover, clad in rugby kit and lined up like a team.
I sing two songs on this record: "Baby, I'm Addicted
to You" and "Song about a Toad" – a sultry ballad
with a punch line. The toad becomes a prince, but
the girl is fed up with princes and wanted a toad all
along. Other treasured moments from cabarets
include Bob singing "I'm the Oldest Cushion-Stuffer
in the Business" and Michael's "Grin", which had
lines in it like:

> *Grin when you're watching King Lear.*
> *Grin when you fall off a pier.*
> *Grin in your trousers, grin in your socks*
> *Grin at the missus when the rent man knocks...*

One way and another, there was an awful lot of
music around all the time. Iwan even wrote a song
about it called "Too Much Music".

# THE FINAL
# YEAR

I was older in my Third Year than in either of the
other two. By this I mean, I calmed down a
little. I found that with a bit of effort, I could
forgo the odd morning coffee in the Playhouse or
the Kemp, and actually stay in my room and work.
Once, I took this to extremes. I had chosen to do a
Special Paper on Marcel Proust and found that the
best and most enjoyable way to get through his
hefty masterpiece was to retire to bed for three days
and read and read. There was a neatness about this
which pleased me. Proust had written *A la
Recherche du Temps Perdu* in his cork-lined bed-
chamber, so I would pay him a kind of compliment
and do the same sort of thing. I imagined that my
room became a kind of Parisian salon ... people
sloped in and out with titbits of gossip and the odd
biscuit, and I did get up at mealtimes and go over
to the dining room to eat. It would take consider-
ably more than a mere work of literature to make
me miss my food.

Blurb writers say: "This book changes lives" with
monotonous regularity but in the case of me and
*A la Recherche...* it really was true. In the slang
current at the time, it "blew my mind". It was "far

out". It was "too much". It really did alter the way
I looked at everything from the moment I read it.
What's more, it's the kind of book you have to read
again once you get to the end, because seeing everything differently now, you want to know what effect
this knowledge has on the text the second time
around. I can't think of another work which so
thoroughly immerses you in an entire society. When
I got up out of bed and started going about my
normal life again, *that* appeared strange to me.

Vince had taken his final exams and left Oxford.
My Couple-dom (Couple-ship? Couple-ness?) was
over. He had never led me to believe that there was
anything permanent about it at all, and I didn't
have any real desire for that kind of relationship
myself. By the time I came back from two weeks in
Corfu with Franny and Dick and Tim and Kathy
(all good friends, that's all), Vince had already
started to go out with someone else. Because I knew
it was coming, so to speak, I wasn't exactly bereft,
but I can remember feeling lonely at the beginning
of the Third Year. Liz had managed to get her love
life sorted out to an admirable degree and had been
a Couple with Graham for a long time. Franny
always had someone to agonize over, and I was, it
seemed, all alone. Moreover, theatrical activity was
going to have to be strictly curtailed if I was to get
any kind of degree at all. I was on the committee
of the ETC and still did some smokers and revues,
but nevertheless, I feared Cocoa in the Evenings if
I didn't do some socializing. Parties had lost their
appeal. They would, at this time of year, be full of
Freshers, eager to impress. I began to feel nostalgic

about *Hang*. Then I remembered Vince's friend Norm, who was doing Postgraduate Research at Nuffield College.

"Go and have a coffee with Norm," Vince had said last year. "He'll be lonely when we all go down."

I sent Norm a postcard. He invited me to tea in Nuffield, and as I'm still married to him, I owe Vince a debt of gratitude for his good idea.

I met all kinds of different people in my last year. I went to dinner in Nuffield and spoke to dauntingly clever ladies who looked like Dowager Duchesses and turned out to be Eminent Economists and Social Historians.

"Reading Spanish," said one such over the braised celery, "how fascinating! I presume you are intending to go into Merchant Banking?" I just smiled and shook my shiny earrings at her. I met people who had nothing to do with the theatre, and best of all, I met Geoff. He was a good friend of Norm's and was going out with (and subsequently married) my old school friend Philippa. It was often impossible to tell if Geoff was joking or serious, which made life difficult. He had the straightest face I'd ever seen. Very tall and thin and fair, he once, in a Chinese restaurant, told me the sad story of his mother being hit on the head by a falling plank while pregnant with his brother, who was then born a dwarf. Norm (also no slouch in the matter of straight faces) confirmed this story. I just wanted to burst out laughing. I *knew* they were pulling my leg – but what if it were true? Wouldn't that be awful? Imagine laughing at Geoff's unfortunate brother! It was hours before I found out the truth. On another occasion, Geoff and Norm played a trick on Philippa and me that lasted the whole day and evening. We were all four spending the weekend in a cottage in Finstock and the two men pretended to quarrel, and then sulked and did not speak to one another for all that time. Philippa and I, desperate for an enjoyable weekend, ran around in small circles trying to get them to make friends and resume normal relations. When they told us what they'd been doing, we nearly went into a genuine sulk of our own.

HOBBES AND LOCKE, ETC.
Final exams at Oxford are called Schools. Schools were approaching, and Liz began to be a little concerned about her Political Theory gobbets. Political philosophers like Hobbes and Locke were all in a dreadful muddle in her head.

"Don't worry," I said. "Norm knows all about those two. He'll help you."

Thus began a series of evenings that I remember as being some of the most enjoyable of all my time at university. Liz's boyfriend, Graham, had a small flat, so we would meet there for dinner once a week. I fancied myself as a cook (Could I have been trying to impress Norm? Maybe.) and used to make huge pots of spaghetti bolognaise, or sometimes fluffy omelettes with French bread and salad, and then after dinner, Norm would talk about Hobbes or whoever was the topic for the evening. Liz took notes. I didn't need to know any of this, but I was spellbound. This was partly Love having its usual effect (see Tim and electric plugs) but it was also amazement at the clarity and concision of everything he said. Liz and I went back to college and I showed her how to write all her notes on one giant sheet. She sailed through her paper with no problems.

DR FAUSTUS

The big theatrical news of 1966 was that Richard Burton and Elizabeth Taylor were coming to star in an OUDS production of *Dr Faustus* at the Playhouse. Professor Neville Coghill was Richard Burton's tutor when Burton was at Oxford and they were still very close. Professor Coghill had the brilliant idea of inviting the Burtons to Oxford. The whole of the theatrical set was in an uproar. Newshounds and paparazzi littered the pavements wherever you went. Everyone but everyone that you could think of was in the production – but not me. It was too near my exams, so sadly I had to watch from the sidelines and eventually from the auditorium. Andreas, the American who played Mephistopheles, was very handsome indeed, and Burton was Burton, with his splendid voice and slightly pock-marked skin. Best of all, though, was Liz, who, as a launcher of a fair number of metaphorical ships in real life, seemed almost typecast as Helen of Troy. Being short and plump myself, I took tremendous comfort in the fact that she was even shorter and a lot plumper. Still, dumpy as she was, her face was beautiful, with almost violet eyes and a very pale skin. I have memories of her in a fur coat.

FOUR DEGREES OVER

I don't know quite how it happened but the Burtons agreed to put money into a show that Woody and

John and Bob were organizing. This was to be a
Musical Revue. I was going to be in it as well. It
would be called *Four Degrees Over* because by the
time the show started, our Four Degrees would be
(yes!) Over.

We were going to open in Oxford, after Schools,
and then take the show on tour to the Mermaid
Theatre in London, then Guildford, Worcester and
eventually the Edinburgh Festival. What we didn't
know was that we would end up at the Fortune
Theatre, Russell Street, in October, thanks again to
Michael Codron. He came to see the show early on,
and liked it a lot, but warned me that I would have
to lose at least a stone before he'd let me on a West
End stage. This meant I had to starve myself all
through the run at Edinburgh, which, considering
that Viv had joined the company specifically to cook
tempting meals, was very cruel. I lived on diet foods
and milk and suffered in the cause of my Art. My
reward for this was that none of the critics called me
"stocky" by the time we opened in London.

We rehearsed the show and studied for Schools at
the same time. It had been written by John and
Woody. Every single musical style that it was possible to parody, we parodied. I had a song where I was
supposed to sound like Edith Piaf, the French singer
of sad love songs, and another where I was dressed
in a man's black tie and tails, like Vesta Tilley the
music hall artiste. Bob did hearty folksongs and a
send-up of a dreadful show then on TV in which people blacked their faces in the manner of Al Jolson,
and sang well-known ditties like "Kemptown
Races", etc. It was called "The Black and White

Minstrel Show". Woody's *tour de force* was a *complete* Gilbert and Sullivan operetta lasting about four minutes in which he sang six different parts in as many voices. Then there were the ensemble numbers: a madrigal, a harmonious setting of phrases from the telephone directory, and best of all, the overture to *Carmen* done entirely in sounds à la Swingle Singers.

When we opened in the West End, an LP was made of the show. We were very proud that George Martin (who produced the Beatles' records) was doing ours as well. I scarcely ever play it now, but I do look at the sleeve sometimes and measure the passage of time. My photo on the back shows me with shoulder-length straight hair, slightly back-combed and turning under at the ends, no glasses and a very low-cut neck to my dress.

SCHOOLS

Of all the traditions surrounding the taking of Schools, the one we attached greatest importance to was The Flower. Your boy/girlfriend was supposed to give you one (thoughtfully bought at a florist's shop and wrapped around the stem with silver foil) either on the evening before your first exam or as you went in on the first morning. By the night before, I hadn't had my flower. I was hoping for a rose, because just a short while ago I pointed out to my botanically illiterate boyfriend just what a rose looked like.

"That's a rose," I said as we went into the quad at Nuffield. "Get one like that."

When I arrived at the Examination Schools, there

everyone was, all dressed up in their black and white like a flock of nervous magpies. Everywhere I looked, there were roses pinned to the lapels of gowns. As well as the magpie-exam-takers, there were all their friends and well-wishers. The crowd was enormous. There was no sign of my beloved. I stretched my neck and peered up the High. Nothing. The first candidates had started to make their way into the building when I saw him and waved. He was sleepy and unshaven, and in his hand was an equally exhausted-looking rose, clearly torn off the nearest Nuffield bush in passing.

"I've been playing poker all night," he explained. "I nearly forgot the rose..." and off he went, to sleep, wishing me luck and putting the bedraggled flower into my hand. I pinned it to my gown and felt just as pleased with it as though it had been one of those slightly artificial-looking blooms usually found in button-holes.

Apart from my Philology paper, which I simply could not do (for the very good reason that I hated Philology and had never so much as opened a book on the subject) I quite enjoyed the exams. The room we sat in was huge. It took ages to walk up to the central invigilators' desk and get more paper. I noticed that Philippa, just as she always had in school, was rushing up to get new supplies to write on before I'd finished my second question. I debated before going in to each exam, doing what Michael-from-Texas had done two years ago: going out for a fag once every hour. This had amused us all greatly when he'd told us about it. An invigilator had had to come with him to make sure he didn't cheat.

There were always bottles of wine and a kind of impromptu party on the pavement after the last papers. I felt relieved that they were over, but was spared the sadness of leaving. First of all there was the show to do at the Playhouse, and then after the summer I would be back, at least at weekends, to see Norm who was in Nuffield for another year. I didn't quite have to face up to Real Life or the Outside World or anything as daunting as that. Not yet.

I got a good Second Class degree. At this time, the record that was being played everywhere was "Help!" by the Beatles. This is the album that has on it my favourite Beatles song. It's called "Yesterday".

POSTSCRIPT

I've only been back to Oxford a couple of times in the last twenty-five years. The town has changed. Carfax is different. They've built a shopping precinct on the Cornmarket. The area behind Pembroke is full of posh shops. I don't mind any of this. The city can take it. It's still just as beautiful as it ever was, although now more people know it is, and the summer, anyway, becomes what Jan Mark has called, in a wonderful story of that name, "Crocodile Time".

Whenever I walk the streets of Oxford now, though, I feel like a ghost. I know everything so well, and yet I am unknown here, unrecognized. All the young people I see (Isn't that Iwan, just disappearing round that corner? And look, there's Franny in that long, trailing skirt, isn't it?) are not my friends, who, like me, are long gone, but strangers young enough to be my children.

Now that I've written this, I'm going to frame the Map and hang it up at last. I shall look at it, and see all of us, my generation, walking along the same streets as the remote illustrious phantoms of Oxford's past.